MI McKIERAN

seasons of a madman

Cover created by Mikey McKieran.

Sheppard Publishing Company

Sheppard Multiverse

First Edition

ISBN 978-0-9952105-9-2

1 2 3 4 5 6 7 8 9 10

Period of Creation: January 2020 – July 2020

TABLE OF CONTENTS

To be read out loud,
at the highest state of inebriation,
in a candlelit room.

FaLL.

autumn
nineteen

As the breath of fall
blows on my exposed skin
I am reminded of
the cold underbelly of this
Otherwise
romantic season.

In fact,
my hands tremble now
as I write this poem.

It almost feels sadistic in a way,
As I blow my nose out,
And you stand by and watch,
laughing a thunderous roar of
rustling leaves.

Oh fall,
A season of such power,
To strip me naked
and leave me wandering
helpless on the streets of
Toronto.

Shall I write to you volatile season?
And if I did,
what would I say?
Damn you?
Damn you.
You did what I feared most.
You made me fall in love.

Love Junkie

Love's a drug I abuse on a daily basis.
The visceral inhalation of your perfume,
the needle-prick kisses you leave on my neck.
I'm a twenty-four-seven junkie.
I wish I could quit you.
Lock myself inside,
barricade the doors.
Get off you cold turkey.

I think about you constantly,
every waking moment.
When I get up,
when I go to sleep.
I need a fix,
I need you to fix me.

The warm embrace in-front of the tele,
Taking hits off your love.
The way you toke, and blow
Kisses at me through the drugstore window.
Riding with me on a carousel of emotions
In a summer night heat.
And I'll spell out,
With my jutted veins
And bruised skin:

I love you.

URBAN JUNGLE

What say you—
Doors of mutable complexity
And wood of tanned divine beauty.

The sexless baroness
Of a cumbersome weight
Tied at the waste,
rattling loudly in unity.

Cicada speak
Lulls me into a dream,
With a mighty cacophony
of symphonic hymns
In the golden gilded linen
I spread across the arid beach
—And lay my wings atop thee.

The symphony of plasma noise
Crunching under restless ponder
And twitchy hands
Pushing button on button
As I make whimsical decision
of the entertainment.

Woman breath, man sweat,
Perennial parental pavilion.
Flower child,
Watch the sun set
And see the truth with me
In a warm embrace.

Urban Jungle. I am here.
You called me. I was awake.
But you already knew that.

GOOD MORNING
(OPEN MOON IRIS)

The iris of an open moon
pupils of complete darkness

Tonight,
I'll walk under your obsidian blanket,
shrouded by mystery.
Streetlight stars.
The howl of madmen.
The rumble of medal steeds
—Now I am truly alive.

Walking calmly through suburbia
like an elusive shadow.
I was. I am.
I know now what makes the city breath.

The thin film of iridescent water
—liquid opal,
caressing my feet
on each step I firmly place
upon the ground.
The wind croons softy against my ear.
The night cry's in ecstasy.
Good morning.

sandpaper
love songs

It's hard to sing love songs
When your voice sounds like sandpaper
And your words cut like ceramic knives.
I wish I could sing to you
With a mellifluous croon
And polished, slippery cords
Instead of hacking out words
Through my cheese grater windpipes.
Maybe the lyrics "I love you"
Sound better out 'another man's mouth
Instead of my own.

What if I lessen my cries?
What if I silence my howls?

whimpering,
Like a wet dog out in the rain.

Would you listen then?

SHE WAS A LIBERTINE.

She was a libertine,
My Queen, my muse
Gone were the days
I'd sing the blues
To her beneath the terrace.

She was my ketamine,
My freedom, my abuse
Gone were the days
Of free love,
A knot becoming loose.

She was my magazine
My preacher, my news
Gone were the days
I'd read to you
Somewhere beneath the terrace.

SLOWLY WATCHING

I watch slowly
As darkness turns nature
Into elegant beasts
That watch me through
The trees.

They sway,
In one unified dance
Choreographed by wind
Lit by moonlight lamps
Flooding light through
The window.

I observe in my private room
In my private box
Faces peering at me
Eyeing me
Watching me
Who does the watching?
Who is on display?

Sleep has become a chore
Nature is my new decor
Evergreen soap operas
Are now my aid in sleep
—The coniferous sandman

I'm currently
on the three a.m. shift
Lying at my "bed post"

Slowly watching.

OH SCENTED IDOLS

Ochre, amber antichrist
Omnipotent candlelight
Operatic effervescent
Ornamental candle scented
Offer for patchouli gods.

Ol' wick in wax a watching
Off the burning storefront awning
O the fiery beast a daunting
Oceans much a quickened calming
Offer for pop icon gods.

Only chants of thunder calling
Only plume or pyre 'a crawling
Over rocks that rock the idols
Opalescent totem smiles
Our scented home among the gods.

Our scented home among the gods.

BEDSIDE
CANDLELIGHT

Perhaps
it is now the bedside candlelight
that warms my body
on a cool summer's eve.

The same light
that draws my attention
away from my suffering
and sorrow.

It is as if a friend is watching over me
—the epicenter of a dancing plume
is but the singular pupil of my most
radiant companion.

Oh, flicker of distraction,
keep me at bay,
hold me ever longer
before I grovel at my body
and ask for forgiveness.

What have I done this time?
What have I done to displease you?

You are but the most mortal deity,
I feed and care for you yet
I still feel your temper,
your rage,
your anger.

Dismiss me of your cruelest intentions
and let me be at peace tonight.

uptown train

Let's take the uptown train.

The same one we took before
parting ways
Oh, so long ago.

And communicate only with
our eyes,
never speaking out loud to
one another.

I'll just rest my head
on your shoulder
in the silence that grows
exponentially louder
as the clickety-clack lulls
me to sleep
and your candle-like heart
flickers next to mine.

WINTER.

DRAWING BLANKS

Drawing blanks in a fit of pain
Contraction, Contraction
Excretion
Retraction.
Why does this occur?
Why is it all the same?
Why do I do this to myself?
Do I like the feeling?
Freed from the mundane
Exquisite pain
The stress-ball squeeze
Release
Please,
stop.

I sit atop my porcelain throne
And wallow
Emptied hollow
Chew and swallow
Down it goes
But what lies
Tongued tied
Still inside
Will come out
And leave me
In silence.

Kamikaze
Stomach

It was as if I had
Swallowed a needle.
No recollection of
My masochism,
Just the not-so-subtle
Reminder, given to me
In sharp but brief
Pinpricks along my abdomen.
I am now at your mercy.
I pray to you
Sideways,
doubled over in your
Unholy strength.
Quivering beneath your
pointed sword.
Or is it I?
The master of my own devices?
The one who deals the damage?
Subconsciously rapping at my insides.
Seldom freed from pain.
Haunted now
By my Kamikaze stomach.

alone
again.

Alone again
In the thick of it all
Stockpiling memories for the
long night ahead of me

Me, myself and I
In total isolation
Left to my own devices
Left to my own worries
Left to my own reflection
Left to lament
Left-handed.

I sigh at the dissolution of
My social connection.
Dreary weather
Metronome rain
To the sad soundtrack
I play tonight.
I am now the singular society
Once part of
The old society.
Twice removed
Estranged
Strange.
Sitting strange in the rain
In the thick of it all
Alone again.

I am worthless,
I am bread.

I am worthless
The on-sale bread
Dismissed by everyone
Lying alone
Untouched
Shaded by my own shadow
Fermenting in my own skin,
At the end of a long market day.

I am alone.
I am different.
I am the multigrain,
Multicolored,
Cinnamon raisin,
Panettone,
Everything bread.

People are afraid to eat me,
Because they don't know
How I'll taste.
I'm am not wonder-bread.
I am not plastic.
I am real.
I am here, right now
Sitting wrapped up and pretty
In front of you —the consumer
—on display.
Am I not good enough for you?
Do I have too many calories?
Do I cost too much?

Why don't you try me?

Why don't you make your way
Over to the sample table
And try a bite?

Why don't you taste
The fucking difference.

I'M THE DAMSEL.

I'm the damsel

—With my locks
And My wire frame
And My pale skin.

I need saving.
I need,
 you.

Locked in the plush tower
Of my mind,
My vices
 —A legion of undead rats
Benign in their slumber
Surround me
And wait
For you to come bursting in
gallantly on horseback
With bright shining armor.

Touch me
Touch me with
your cold dead hands
Kiss me with your chapped lips
And chipped cream teeth
Holster your glass sword,
And carry me home.

Love's own Refugee

And so,
it continues...

the pail overcast of a new damage,
Following me down the steps
into frozen morning.

With clear yolk
running down my
freezer-burnt nose,
And a dull cough,
displacing air for sickened moisture.

The grumble
of an early morning empty
vibrates up along my chest
and manifests itself as a benign worry,
turning the gears in an unnecessary panic.
Hopelessness is kept hidden.

Vile, caustic hands of self-harm lie trembling
in a shadowed corner,
twitching like a wasp in quiet anger.

You were,
you weren't,
you peered into my epidermal windows,
holding my hands
and whispering commands in my
sunken ears.

Are you full yet?

Feeding off me while I sleep
silently in my depression.

You have a way of sneaking in,
like a rat hiding from a summers rain.
Love's own refugee.

PERSONAL
RAG DOLL

Wet canine in a two by two box.
You're filth,
sickness,
and pure evil.

And I love you for it.

In some twisted way I love you.

Every whip you crack over my back,
every nail you drive into my hand,
every goddamn insult
you spit from your wretched tongue.

I love you.
I love you like the fresh pain of
boiling oil
over naked feet.
I love you like a finger over sawblade.

I'm your personal rag doll.
Love ain't love till you draw a little blood.
Let's kiss and makeup
and we can be blood buddies.
You can move me like your puppet.

Happier
Without You

I was happier without you
Parasitic, posthumous,
person of interest
person of my interest
Rising from the dead,
casting spells on mad men
A ghost of my forgotten love
Haunts me softly,
Holds me close in a
bone dry embrace.

Whisper sweet nothing's in my ear,
A catatonic love stare,
An invisible kiss.

The catalyst
that was your inevitable change,
Like flipping effortlessly
through a photo-book of memories,
The carousel of frozen happiness,
Is now an empty shell
Of your former self.

meat vessel

My body hates me.

I am captain of a ship
that desperately wants to sink.

It wants to hit the iceberg.
It wants to take me down with it.

It's drawn to pain
Like flies drawn to lightbulbs.
I perspire sorrow.
I metabolize suffering.

Contrary to sunflowers,
I am of dour complexion.
In charge of a sensitive
Meat vessel.
watching it closely
—Like a nanny
To make sure it does not
injure itself.
I am grasping at every
Little bit of authority
I still have left.

I am in control.
I am in control.

DEAR ANXIETY

Thank you for sitting on my chest,
like a two-year-old child,
still stuck on infantile sadism.

And for the constant death threats
that have me walking like a cautious dog,
a noosed collar around my trembling neck.

I really don't enjoy the stomach squeezes or
The constant tugging at my face,
the twitches from my eye to mouth or
my heart skipping beats
like improv'd jazz.

And the way you follow me everywhere
and scare me just for fun
Like two children walking home from school,
is frankly, quite childish.

You've damaged me in ways
I cannot express
yet I'm forever in your debt.
And I hate myself for
allowing this toxic relationship to continue,
but I'm worried if I lose you

I'd be nothing.

Like a Rose

I'm glad my pain amuses you.

Now watch my body shrivel
As the seams around my skin unglue
And the flesh between my organs drizzle.

And I collapse here on the floor,
the vibrant red of pedals torn
that wash away the aches and pain.

Like a rose I'll rise again.

PSYCHOSOMATICS

A thought more powerful than free will
An itch, a scratch, a trick.
A simple manifestation
of something that does not exist.
Like self-magic,
A check, resist
mind games that'll drive rationality away;

A hurt sore, revolving door
Of psychosomatic symptoms.

A new death, a new rest
A catatonic act in jest;
Self diagnose an empty mirage
The illusion of a rigid mental state

A cold clasp, a new gasp
A religious check in this new paranoia
Toiling at a false assurance
The blunt whisper of fear
And the assessment of nothing.

The quick heal, the new feel
The appetite of knowledge,
The mental cloak of sanity,
as I relax the grip
and mutter mantras under
recovered breath.

The keep cool, the new fool
The mastermind behind the plot
A vile, old sensation locked deep
In a mental box.

WORLD'S GREATEST ACTOR

I'm the world's greatest actor.
I know this because others think I'm happy.

***

I've got the best fake smile in the game.
It works so well I make a whole
fourteen dollars an hour.
It works so well I get free hugs.

I practice my smile in the mirror.
First, I relax all the muscles in my face,
and then in a big burst of energy
stretch my mouth out
from ear to ear.
I hold this pose
until my muscles give out,
letting my stretched skin fall back
into a melancholy curl,
like a new elastic band trying to
retain its shape.

It's all a big facade.

I have five shows a week,
eight hours a day,
each show more stressful than the last.
Like a rock stuck in a rapid stream
I am slowly eroding
day after day,
show after show.

I'm lucky though,
I get to pick my costume every morning.

What tie will I wear?
And with what pair of shoes?

Sometimes I get lost in character
and begin to believe
I'm actually enjoying myself.

Little slip ups like that humor me.

HOLY CANDLE

holy candle, burn so bright
burn so short in evening light
with brandy stains, a half-dimed rein
over many a troubled people.

holy rope, wrapped oh so tight
a dangling darling in evening light
with jugular strains, and candied veins
oh lord, the pressured people.

holy silence, sleep at night
thoughts a turning, hurting fright
with choice in hand, a test of might
oh god, please save the people.

watch me sleep (in fear)

I fear sleep.
Every second,
every minute,
every little tick on the old grandfather.

It is a great marathon of the mind.
To slow down such fiery steeds in mental molasses.
To calm a cacophony of internal sounds.

Keep me to the brink of daylight.
Keep me to the brink of madness.
Tease me and toy me like your own personal puppet,
You sandman,
Sadist, sovereign fuck.

God bless you silicon sneeze man
God help me silicon, please man.
Please man!
Let go the grip of terror.
Leave me to tranquil slumber!
Oh, the cumbersome grog
Of a half sleep, of a half peace.

Watch me function on your small gifts.
Your sleep sample platters.
I'll scavenge on the minutes you give me.
Watch me sleep.
Watch me.
 Sleep.

SPRiNG.

FLies

Watching the cheap kettle
boil a thick,
black,
carcinogenic fume
that clouds over the entire kitchen,
filling crack after crack
with a gray fog,
leaving a thin film of
molten plastic atop every surface
in a five-foot radius.
I am the fly on the wall.
The small,
elusive bug that observes
only with compound eyes.
No one notices me,
no one interacts with me.

Two lovers
in a back alley parking lot,
making drunken love
behind club doors
as they fuck each other
like animals in heat,
howling madly
at a poor virgin moon,
—forced to watch until
sun breaks the horizon.
I am the fly on the wall.
Moonlight reflecting off my hairy,
iridescent skin
as I maniacally rub my hands together
and buzz my wings
violently in arousal.

An old man
sitting on a rickety white spoke chair,
eating raw meat off a
ceramic plate.
His elbows pressed hard against
the old oak table,
a newspaper in hand,
spread out
taut and parallel
to his weathered chest.
He pushes thick glasses
up against his crooked nose
and leaves to use the bathroom.
I am the fly on the wall.
Crawling
slowly across stained wallpaper,
teasing my conscious at the mere thought
of impregnating raw meat
with my offspring.

Two friends
playing catch in a
summer school yard,
fighting over
the adolescent question of
"who's better than who".
Hysterical yelling,
taunt and tantrum.
I am the fly on the wall.
I'm growing older now
and can no longer
humor myself sadistically
at the misery of others.

Two men,
sitting in silence,

across a crimson casket.
clouds expel small teardrops
that pitter-patter
along the shingled roof.
I patiently wait in silence.
Hardly noticed,

I am the man on the wall.

mannequin
BRiDe

Mannequin bride,
Oh, how I love you.

But recently
I find we've grown apart.
You no longer laugh at my jokes
and when we fight you
never respond.

I know you still love me
because you smile
everywhere we go,
but I'm slowly watching us
grow distant.

I've tried bringing us to a
relationship counselor,
but you refuse to sit down
whenever asked.
I don't know why you need to
be so stubborn.
It embarrasses me.

My friends make fun of you.
They objectify you.
I hate it.
If they can't love you
they can't love me either.

They call you things like
dummy,
plastic woman.

They say you're worth
three hundred tops.

Don't listen to 'em,
I think you're priceless.

I remember
the first time
I met your friends.

They were working at
Victoria Secret.
Standing there in the window
like some sort of
red light
district
display.

Men drooling over them.

I don't know why they can't have
a job with dignity.
At least you worked at Banana Republic.

My parents don't really approve of you.
They call me insane,
delusional.
They tell me to go find a "real girl".
It's just their conservative thinking.
They'll warm up to you.

Sex.
Sex is a different story.
There's no passion anymore.
It feels cold and fake.
I don't know what you like

and what you don't
because either way
you're speechless.

I wish you'd just love me,
hold me,
Once more.

Gimme that rigor-mortis love.

STATION DELAY

The writhing tendrils
of a quick display of pain
And the push
And the sting
Of one thousand firecrackers
going off below

Steam hissing out the ol' tailpipe.

Time has now emptied
the passengers
from the chassis

And the train begins
moving once more.

3:20am

WaLL BOY

There's a boy within these walls
Living, breathing,
whisper-talking
I can hear his nimble walking
in between
The Plastered walls.

I can hear his tiny feet
Pitter patter down the hall
A thousand tiny steps is all
Nothing more, but if we meet
Staring at me, over sheets
Breathing softly as he seats
Himself next to me
Sitting small.

I can't recall the meaning
For this unexpected greeting
By the boy who lives within the walls
Sitting quiet, sitting small.

Black as night inside my room
It all was silent hitherto
Now the boy is oddly present
Breathing on me, not as pleasant
Disturbing sleep that I could use
Aloud he ponders, soft he croons
Out my chamber, gone so soon
He whispers loudly down the halls
Finally finding,
prying, spying

Watching silent, analyzing
Peering through a tiny view
In my old and plastered walls.

WHAT LURKS BENEATH

What lurks beneath
The wooden structure
Lined with brick and drywall
Where I lay my head.

Tis a thought to ponder nightly
as I slip into my bed.

But as my ponder slowly fades
The house I slumber slowly wakes
And roars a mighty waking yawn
That decimates the silent space

How late!
You shout at morning like a cock
It's time to sleep, you've woken me
Your noise must stop, no hesitance
Stop the metal rattle
Up along the iron vents.
Ringing like an iron bell
Ringing like the gates of hell
Louder now then ever
Would you please
Oh pretty please

shut
The fuck up.

—And let me get some rest.

Thank you.

THE BUZZ

The slippery tongues of caustic love
both seduce and seclude me
from the false reality
I've grown to admire.

Day-glow buzz on Honeybee love.
Moist body against body.
Teat on teat.
Sucking off the breast of mother earth.
A human wave gyrating to
the audio fuel for summer's love.

Don't hate me, Haight-Ashbury.
Kiss me under psychedelic suns
and ethereal transient clouds.
Kaleidoscopic eyes beckon me with
"come hither" glances.
The silence between us screams.
Baptize me in your holy affection.
Let me warship you.
Let me call you god.
Free me from pain,
and I'll read your
scripture like religion.

Yuppie Coffee Table Book

Hey.
Hey you.
Yes. You.
Can you help me?
Can you do me a favor?
Can you get me the fuck off this table?

I've been stuck on here for weeks.
It's quite boring.
I'm so lonely.
No one ever reads me.
I thought that's the whole point of a book
—*is to be read.*
However, here I am.
Untouched. Quite virgin.
Still smelling like glossy bleached paper
and the overstock backroom
of Barnes and Noble.

Sometimes I wish I could be their checkbook.
That book gets touched often.
The little bank-papered nymphomaniac.
Jeez. I just want to be used!

The company they invite over
won't even read me.
But they sure as hell
like to reference me in their conversations
every ten minutes.
And for gods sakes,
I'm not a fucking coaster,
don't put your

Folgers cup of shit on my pristine,
Clean
Glossy
Saucy
hardcover!

I wish someone else,
anyone else would have bought me.
But I guess that's a hard ask
when your name is
Yuppie Coffee Table Book.

BOTOX

I'm flush in the face
Stretched tight like a canvas.
I'm practically plastic,
elastic and sanded.

I'm your mother's upholstery,
Your father's new handbag,
I'm leathered and weathered
For only two ninety-five and

I don't feel a thing,
no nothing at all.
You can slap me and pinch me
I could fall a great fall.
When I go for a ride
With the wind in my hair
And formaldehyde skin
buffed and shined with great care,

I'm on my way to the doc
For my new rhinoplasty
It's just the newest procedure

For this ol' human taxidermy.

asbestos bread

Oh, what a time I'm having,
baking myself some
asbestos bread.
I only recently came up with the idea,
after accidentally bumping the broom
into my eighteenth-century wall,
and then came a crack,
and then a rumble
and then the whole goddamn thing
fell right into my kitchen.

And when I saw it there,
lying next to the
milk and eggs
I realized
that asbestos looks
a lot like flour.
And so, I added it in.
And my god,
I'm glad I made the switch.

It has a bit more fiber than
whole grain
but not the density,
and the amazing feeling you get
when you bite off a chunk and chew.
It makes these little gashes
in your gums and throat,
quite a unique
and wonderful experience really.
Nothing like it.

And if pain is pleasure,
well then,
I'm creaming my pants!

But the thing I don't
particularly like
about my new-found
asbestos bread
is when I have to use the washroom in
the morning.

It's quite comparable to
the feeling of loosely running
a long sheet of twenty grit sandpaper
along the inside of your
rectal wall.

It's like a desert down there;
the wild, wild west,
but that's alright,
because I'm sitting down now,
with my friends,
and we're all eating asbestos bread
on a sunny afternoon.

new coat

I got myself a new coat.
Actually,
it's quite old.
Consider it,
"newly thrifted".
Black polyester
lined vertically with buttons
—stained with the blood,
Sweat
and tears
of each body
that rode this saddle-stitched steed
before me.

The stains represent a sort of
twisted status,
like I'm the new filth
in a long line of past generations.
And so, I decide to flaunt
each stain like:

1. a militant's badge

2. a human trophy,
super-soaked like
a summer camp tie-dye

3. a soluble sticker
displayed dashingly dapper
on my breast pocket.

It's like a wearable art gallery.
A set of cured,
liquid pictures

on a fibrous frat wall.
And if I could,
I'd label each stain by year,
Artist
and medium.

i.e. Nineteen seventy-six,
Jerry Jamethson,
semen.

Consider me an art collector.

My new coat is quite large.
It gives the sweet illusion of
self confidence.
It hides the sour scent
of fear.
Sometimes I forget I'm me
and slip into a sort of character
—Sherlock, Rorschach, Neo.
And for a brief moment in time,
I'm cured.
My new,
wearable,
antique antibiotic.

On the cold mornings,
every commute begins to
feel like a play.
The long honks and grunts
are the soundtrack
to a great and wonderful comedy.
Each interaction becomes
a new scene
and sometimes
I scramble to remember the words
in the script I'd learned

so many years ago.

When I'm home; however,
I'm me.
And as I sink myself
Into the corduroy couch,
I am brought back to the sweet
unimportance of it all.

THE FALCON

There once was a child
They called him
the falcon.

He was a scrawny boy,
Short, small and mellow
But he was a curious fellow
And he wanted to fly.

So, he climbed a big building
That touched the sky
And he was certain that flapping
His wings like a bird
Would make him
fly through the sky
But then it occurred

That it doesn't.

YOU'RE NOT GWYNETH PALTROW

Plastered walls
and old oak baseboards.
The door swings open
and a woman dressed in
a plain white robe
greets me.
She lives across the hall.
I can see her
eyeing me like a wild cat,
hungry and vicious.
Our eyes lock.

She says "hi",
"how are you"
and "nice to meet you"
all in a ten-foot stare.
God, she fucks me up.

She beckons me with
her slender finger
and I cautiously trot
towards her.

Her perfume
was like a slap across the face
and a hard kiss on the lips;
punch drunk love baby.

She twirls her hair a little,
and then,

with a hard grasp around my shirt collar,
she pulls me in.
Our heads connect,
her mouth is up against my ear.

"Do you know who I am?"
she asks in a seductive voice.

"No", I reply in a volatile response.

She brings me closer and whispers,
"I'm Gwyneth Paltrow ".

I look at her the way a foreigner looks at
a foreign menu.

"You are not Gwyneth Paltrow".

Two weeks later we are on a date.
I am biting down hard on
a piece of sourdough bread.
She is having chicken noodle soup.
Her eyes twinkle in the mood lighting.
We are in love.
It is our two-week anniversary.
I made her a homemade card,
I bought her a cake.
I motion at the waiter
and he brings out
the cake from the fridge.
He displays it on the table.
She smiles for a second and then
she frowns.
She wipes her hand
across the top of the cake,
wiping off all the words
I've intricately written in icing.

She motions at the waiter
and he brings her a piping tube.
She writes on the cake,

"Gwyneth Paltrow".

I look down at what she wrote
and then back at her.

"You are not Gwyneth Paltrow".

Three days later we are having sex.
Her body is firmly atop mine.
She moans a little.
She calls me Chris Martin.
I am not Chris Martin.
Royal Tenenbaums
is playing in the background.
The same white robe she wore
is lying disheveled on my
bedroom floor.
My bookshelves are lined with movies,
some of these include:

Shakespeare in Love,
Sliding doors
and Iron Man Three.
I make a note of them as she climaxes.

She screams in ecstasy,
and as if it were her dying breath,
she moans in my ear:
"I'm Gwyneth Paltrow".

summer.

TWENTY-TWENTY, THE PERSONAL

(An attempt at verbal acrobatics)

I'm the baby faced
new raced
Halfie Halfling
Barely five foot five
Took a height dive
at puberty's end
And never started growing.

Then became the
Caucasian
Canadian
Asian mixed smoothie of:
One-part (I)talian
One-part (you)talian
One-part canto-cantered
Baby handed
bachelor boy
who could
Barely hold a c minor.

Kinder than the
new brute ivy-league
daddy please-ing
manny fanny of today's society.

Superficial
Falatial Falacio
free frolic
Even flow
of Eddie Vedder's lost tongue
from the neat

dip and dive of my scratched up
record collection
or the recollection
of when music was good.

Misunderstood was my daily motto,
legato speak for those who
didn't "get me"
lefty freak,
said he who didn't understand,
speaking bland tongues
to the new clique.

Last week
I sat at home and listened to
Morrison in my left ear,
Lennon in my right ear,
a personal whisper
" ménage et trois"
looking myself in the mirror
and faux smiling in despair
as my hairs stand on end
and I stare silently at
my hundred-pound body
standing curved
like a human toothpick,
bent in a test of force,
barely resting as I walk canted,
loose lips slanted in a twisted pout.

New sprouts
spout street slang in verbal combat,
hardline handwriting
in twenty first century cuneiform
 —or that's what it looks like
to me, see, I'm so far from the norm,
two streets apart,

my style rests in the past,
worn last year's model
way before that.

The black sheep
steeped in the wet dream
of modern-day society,
divided from the peers
that walk beside me.

Sobriety is the difference
between me and you,
I choose the former,
looking over, cold shoulder
face forward and carry on.
The wrong side
or the new pride
of being different,
the twenty twenty, the personal.

ten o' seven

Pressing two fingers against my temples
as my roommate fucks in the adjacent room,
in this putrid god-awful sin-filled city.

Lead lungs from smoking,
Iron gut from canned tuna.
And the fact that I'm ten stories up
doesn't help either.

I'm not afraid of heights,
But rather,
Afraid of what I might do
when I inch myself closer and closer
towards the balcony.
For my thoughts have more strength
Than my muscles.

With a firm grip,
Jacking off to vintage magazines
'cause the internet is broken
and I can't afford to fix it.

Sitting ass naked
on my living room couch
'cause all my clothes are in the wash
And my legs ache from
frequent nomadic trips
around the city.

Spooning pillows,
'cause I'm two thousand kilometers away
from my lover
and I rather buy food than gas.

Waking up at two in the afternoon
because there are no windows
And the sun is now but a mere figment of my
imagination.

Sunken eyes, tattered flannel,
Sipping coffee after coffee
till my teeth stain brown.
Washing hand after hand till my skin rubs dry
Because everything is dirty
And I wish to be clean.

Laugh Like a madman.

Laugh like a madman
As everyone you loved
Desserts you.

Laugh like a madman
As the pale facade lifts
The mask from its twitching
Face.

Laugh like a madman
As you slam your fragile head
Across oak banisters
And shout great anti-hymns
In strange tongues
And rip the tight-gripped cords
From your throat!

Deceit! Deceit!
Lies callused over by your
Worthless words.
Greet me eye to eye
So I can spit in your face
And hack blood on your forehead.
Pissant scholar brethren.

How much blood should I draw
To become one of you?
How deep should I cut
So I can laugh with you
At our nine to five suffering.
Bring me your head,
Your

—corporate taxidermy,
Your putrid conformity
You yuppie bunch of
Bigoted mongrels.

I'll watch you choke on
Your smog
I'll watch you bet on your
Cock stocks
I'll watch you choke
On checkbook ejaculate
And when we meet eye to eye
Once more
I'll give you the kiss of change

And laugh like a madman.

ABOUT THE AUTHOR

Mikey McKieran is a Canadian poet,
songwriter, filmmaker, writer and
visual artist.

InDex of
FiRST Lines

Printed in Great Britain
by Amazon

67181700R00047